Color Yourself to
MINDFULNESS

100 mandalas and motifs
to color in to reduce stress

CICO BOOKS
LONDON NEW YORK

Published in 2015 by CICO Books
An imprint of Ryland Peters & Small Ltd
20–21 Jockey's Fields   341 E 116th St
London WC1R 4BW   New York, NY 10029
www.rylandpeters.com

10 9 8 7

A CIP catalog record for this book is available from
the Library of Congress and the British Library.

US ISBN (**Color Yourself to Mindfulness**):
978 1 78249 323 5

UK ISBN (**Colour Yourself to Mindfulness**):
978 1 78249 325 9

Printed in China

Illustration: Stephen Dew
Adapted from original artworks by
Melissa Launay

Senior editor: Carmel Edmonds
In-house designer: Fahema Khanam
In-house design assistant: Kerry Lewis
Art director: Sally Powell
Head of production: Patricia Harrington
Publishing manager: Penny Craig
Publisher: Cindy Richards

CONTENTS

4

PASSION

GROWTH

CHILDHOOD

GRACE

8

WISDOM

PLENTY

MENTOR

SERVICE

DIVINE LOVE

DEVOTION

BELTANE

15

MIDSUMMER

OSTARA

MABON

WILLOW KNOT

THE GREEN MAN

THE SOLAR WHEEL

SUCCESS

DANCE

NEW JOURNEY

INVOCATION

FORGIVENESS

GROUNDING

PAIN

INTEGRATION

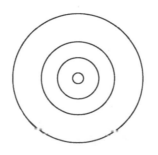

REACHING OUT

SELF-ESTEEM

AWARENESS

LAUGHTER

THE MAZE

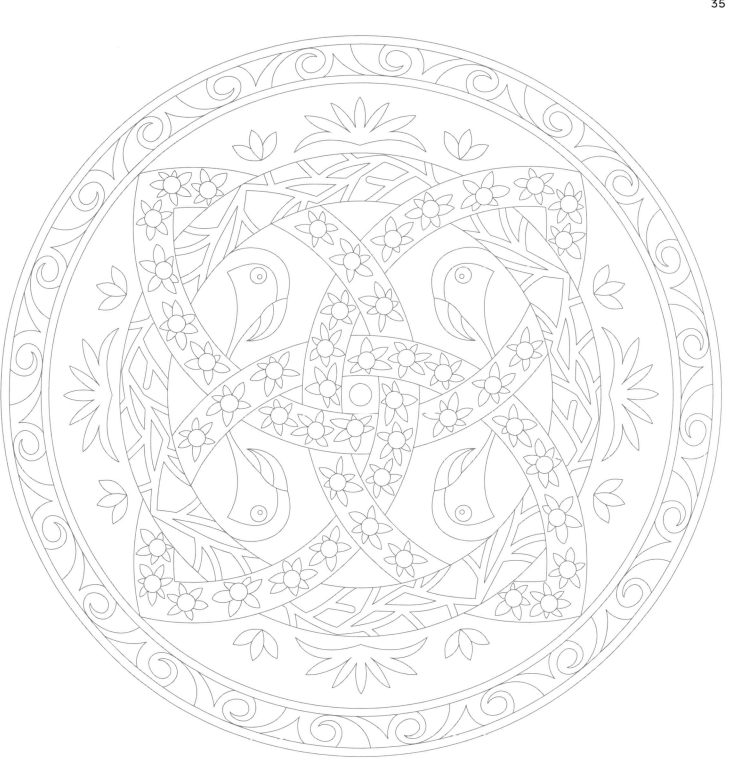

COMMUNICATION

LOSS

HEALING

FLOW

PLANTING THE SEED

COMPLETION

SHRI YANTRA

THE HANDS OF GOD

MASCULINITY

44

CONNECTION

FLOWER KNOT

COMPASSION

TREE OF LIFE

48

LOOKING ANEW

ENERGY

50

KARMA

DEPRESSION

ABUNDANCE

PEACE

COMPANIONSHIP

EARTH

BOREDOM

NEW THINGS

CREATIVITY

KNOWLEDGE

RENEWAL

RELEASE

PERSONAL POWER

WATER OF LIFE

GUILT

NATURE

RAINBOW

NEW LIFE

CORNUCOPIA

RIVERS

NEW BEGINNINGS

BLISSFUL DESIRE

SELF-EXPRESSION

BONDING

76

NATURE SPIRITS

IMPERMANENCE

LOOKING

RITUAL

LOVE

WHEEL OF LIFE

FEMININITY

EARTHLY CONNECTION

84

CONCEPTION

MOUNTAIN

DEITY ANGEL

GRIEF

WATER

BOUNTIFUL

SUFFERING

CHILDREN

CHAKRA

MEDITATION

DOODLE YOUR OWN MANDALA

To make your own mandala, sit peacefully and quieten your mind. You can copy the motifs here or from throughout the book. Alternatively, create your own, such as stars, crescent moons, suns, flowers, and shapes linked with the elements (earth, air, fire, and water).